T0318859

THE RISE AND PROGRESS OF
CLASSICAL ARCHAEOLOGY

THE RISE AND PROGRESS OF CLASSICAL ARCHAEOLOGY

WITH SPECIAL REFERENCE TO THE UNIVERSITY OF CAMBRIDGE

An Inaugural Lecture

BY

ARTHUR BERNARD COOK

LAURENCE PROFESSOR OF
CLASSICAL ARCHAEOLOGY

CAMBRIDGE
AT THE UNIVERSITY PRESS
1931

CAMBRIDGE
UNIVERSITY PRESS

University Printing House, Cambridge CB2 8BS, United Kingdom

Cambridge University Press is part of the University of Cambridge.

It furthers the University's mission by disseminating knowledge in the pursuit of education, learning and research at the highest international levels of excellence.

www.cambridge.org
Information on this title: www.cambridge.org/9781316613122

© Cambridge University Press 1931

First published 1931
First paperback edition 2016

A catalogue record for this publication is available from the British Library

ISBN 978-1-316-61312-2 Paperback

THE RISE AND PROGRESS OF
CLASSICAL ARCHAEOLOGY

SIR JAMES JEANS has recently been explaining to us the cosmic process by which planets and their satellites came to be. Something analogous, I take it, happens in the normal development of any important subject. Under the strong compelling influence of Science the study of Classics, for example, has already been drawn out into a series of peripheral studies, *A, B, C, D, E*, which have taken shape as Literature, Philosophy, History, Archaeology, and Language. And these in their turn are beginning to throw off satellites of their own—Epigraphy, Papyrology, and the like.

I am concerned with a small section only of this great mental movement. My business is to set out as simply as possible the successive stages through which Classical Archaeology has hitherto passed, to indicate its present position, and to form some tentative forecast of its future growth. In so doing I shall have to touch—I hope, with reverent fingers—on the work of not a few honoured names. For this, like all or nearly all of our Cambridge Schools, has been built upon personalities. It is the old story of individual interest, individual devotion, individual sacrifice. A long list of whole-hearted workers has surveyed the field, has dug the foundations, has erected the scaffolding, and course by course has reared the fabric. One thinks of Colvin, and Clark, and Walston, and Middleton, and Ridgeway, and Sandys. And now at the last Sir Perceval Maitland Laurence by his far-sighted and open-handed bequest has given to their construction a stability and a permanence, for which all lovers of the subject must be profoundly grateful. The best justification of his munificence in an age of enforced economy will be a history, however hasty, of the cause that he had at heart.

Classical Archaeology as we understand the term (and I will not be inveigled into defining it) was a product of the Italian Renaissance. Petrarch in a letter[1] to Cardinal Colonna—written, I suppose, in that fine script of his from which our printed italics are derived[2]—tells how he took a ramble through the ruins of Rome, identifying places familiar to him in legend or history but forgotten, as he complains, by the Romans themselves:

Here was the palace of Evander—here the temple of Carmentis—here the cave of Cacus—here the fostering She-wolf and the Fig-tree called *Ruminalis* or more accurately *Romularis*.

He runs on in this rapid allusive style, noting temples and tombs:

Here Caesar triumphed; here Caesar fell.

He hurries us past arches and porticoes, columns and statues, pagan and Christian memorials of all sorts. He makes mistakes, of

[1] Petrarch *epist. de rebus familiaribus* 6. 88.
[2] Sir J. E. Sandys *A History of Classical Scholarship* Cambridge 1908 ii. 99.

course, and Lanciani[3] would minimise his merits. But, having been long at the business, I confess to a sympathy with people who make mistakes. And, after all, there is no mistaking a man's enthusiasm, let alone a poet's. In another letter[4] he tells us that, during his stay in Rome, he used to buy oddments brought him by the peasants:

Often some vineyard-digger would come to me with an ancient gem in his hand, or some gold or silver coin, damaged now and again by the hard tooth of his mattock. He would ask me to buy the thing, or else to puzzle out the features of its portrait-head.

These coins meant much to Petrarch. On the strength of them he urged[5] Charles IV to copy the medallic art of his predecessors, the Roman emperors, and so started modern medallists on the road which led them first to imitate and then to surpass the ancients themselves.

Petrarch's enthusiasm was contagious. Poggio Bracciolini, the famous Florentine scholar,

[3] R. Lanciani *Ancient Rome in the light of recent Discoveries* London 1888 p. 1 ff.

[4] Petrarch *op. cit.* 18. 8.   [5] *Id. ib.* 19. 3.

saw the ruins of Rome becoming yet more ruinous, and detailed their decay in his treatise *On Fortune's Changes*. An initial from that work preserves Poggio's portrait. He himself wrote a beautiful book-hand, and acted as papal secretary for fifty years. It was for Pope Nicolas V that he produced his translation of Diodorus; and another manuscript initial shows him presenting the work to his patron. In his house at Rome Poggio had a chamber, which he called his *Gymnasiolum*, crowded with a collection of statues, marble heads, gems, and coins. All the heads were noseless and most of them deplorably mutilated. But Poggio had insight enough to recognise their beauty, and great was his joy when Master Donatello himself dropped in and praised one of his treasures. In 1427 we find him planning to build in his garden at Terranuova a small Gallery for his antiquities and to combine with it a Library for his manuscripts—in short, to construct the first Museum of Classical Archaeology. All honour to Poggio! Nor did he confine his efforts to Italy. Friends from Rhodes helped him to further acquisitions. In Chios he heard of three marble heads—a Juno, a Minerva, and a Satyr—said to be by Polykleitos and Praxiteles. But Poggio was cautious and remembered that their vendor was a Greek!

Meantime others were hard at work collecting inscriptions. Cola di Rienzo as early as 1344 was deciphering records on marble and bronze. To him we owe the very first collection of Latin epitaphs. He also discovered an important decree relating to Vespasian, and ventured to expound the same—though he rather spoilt his exposition by taking *pomerium* to mean 'apple-orchard'![6] Ciriaco, who came of a mercantile family in Ancona, was—like Schliemann—a self-taught student of Latin and Greek. He travelled, for trading purposes, far and wide through the Levant. We hear of him in Alexandria, Cilicia, Bithynia, Rhodes, Chios, Samos, Sicily, Dalmatia—even as far afield as Beirut and Damascus. Everywhere with om-

[6] R. Lanciani *op. cit.* p. 6f. H. Dessau *Inscriptiones Latinae selectae* no. 244, 15.

nivorous zeal he made a point of copying Greek and Latin inscriptions, and so put together in a sense the first *Corpus*—three vast and rather miscellaneous manuscript volumes, of which fragments only are now extant. But they suffice to prove his painstaking fidelity. In Rhodes he discovered an inscription in Doric lettering. In Egypt he copied hieroglyphs from the Great Pyramid. And he rightly lays stress on inscribed records as more trustworthy evidence than the manuscript tradition. Larfeld does not hesitate to speak of Ciriaco as the father of modern Greek epigraphy.[7]

To lengthen this list of names would be easy. But I have said enough to show that already, five hundred years ago, the humanists of Italy had made a beginning, a good beginning, with most branches of Classical Archaeology. The fact is, as Symonds puts it, 'The men of that nation and of that epoch were bent on creating a new intellectual atmosphere for

[7] W. Larfeld *Handbuch der griechischen Epigraphik* Leipzig 1907 i. 30.

Europe by means of vital contact with antiquity'.[8] *Vital* contact. This implies that they endeavoured, not merely to appreciate, but actually to live, the life of the ancients. They wanted to forget the dark ages and to bring again the brightness of imperial Rome. They were prepared to talk Latin and on great occasions to wear a laurel-wreath. In this vein the architects of the Italian Renaissance attempted to revive the Roman orders, even if they had to be superposed upon a Gothic structure. New combinations of classical features were encouraged, and discrepancies could always be masked by a wealth of decorative detail. Vitruvius, neglected in his own day, awoke to posthumous fame. And the veriest dullard could see that St Peter's dome was but a converted Pantheon.

How much, or how little, of all this galvanised and rather factitious classicism found its way to Cambridge? The British, as Boccaccio laments, were 'slow to learn' (*studiis*

[8] J. A. S[ymonds] in the *Enc. Brit.*[11] xxi. 891.

tardusque Britannus).[9] But I doubt if Boccaccio did much to help them. His manual of mythology was not easy reading, and the early editions of Hyginus offered a disconcerting blend of classical text with medieval woodcuts. However, the British at least possessed a saving sense of humour. Hence they did not adopt the extravagances of the ultra-classical movement, and—if Archaeology affected them at all—it was in a purely external fashion. Cambridge has college-buildings of Elizabethan date that exhibit not a few Vitruvian traits— the First Court of Sidney Sussex, the Second Court of St John's, above all the Nevile Court of Trinity. Earliest, and in some ways most interesting, of the series is the triad of Gateways possibly designed and certainly erected by Dr Caius. The Gate of Honour, as it originally stood,[10] will illustrate my point. Its four-centred arch is of course a perpendicular

9 Boccaccio *Lettere* ed. Corazzini p. 243, cp. p. 363 *serus Britannus*.
10 R. Willis and J. W. Clark *The Architectural History of the University of Cambridge* Cambridge 1886 i. 177 fig. 9.

feature thoroughly characteristic of the period. But almost everything else is in the would-be classical style. We see a Roman triumphal arch surmounted by a Roman temple and topped by a Roman tomb. Pelion, Olympus, Ossa! But the critical eye does not at once detect the incongruities, because attention is distracted by the decorative adjuncts—shields and pyramids, obelisks and sun-dials, not to mention the serpent and dove which crown the whole symbolic edifice. Could anything be more eloquent of the age that produced it?

Anglo-classic architects of the next century or so dispensed with unnecessary complications and fell back upon a purer Roman style. Here again Cambridge can boast magnificent examples—Sir Christopher Wren's great Library at Trinity, or a little later James Gibbs' half-finished Senate House and the glorious block at King's that bears his name. Petrarch and his peers would have been proud to go in and out amid such surroundings. Yet, if we are honest with ourselves, we must admit that even these masterpieces here and there have failed to catch the true classical spirit. Architecture? Yes. But what of architectural sculpture? Wren proposed to adorn his Library with four plaster statues, and—said he—'there are Flemish artists that doe them cheape'.[11] In the end Gabriel Cibber carved the figures of Divinity, Law, Physic, and Mathematics, which still stand above the balustrade: I confess, they leave me cold. More attractive are the relief-panels on the beautiful bridges of Clare and St John's. Those at St John's have never been published. They show Father Neptune flanked by Water-babies with mirror, shell-trumpet, and sea-wrack; and again 'Camus, reverend sire', with a pile of books above him and the Johnian buildings, bridge and all, in the background. The designs—sanctioned perhaps by Wren— are deserving of study; but, since they face outward over the river, they are hard to see, and, mindful of the warning *sexagenarios de ponte*, I gave up the attempt in favour of a telephotic lens. The reliefs on the Clare Bridge face inwards and are much more noticeable,

[11] T. D. Atkinson *Cambridge* London 1897 p. 448 n. 2.

stimulus of nascent Science—to realise that they lived in a very interesting world and that life, even local life, had a long history behind it. The Age of Antiquaries had arrived.

Their forerunner was Sir Thomas Browne, 'Doctour of Physick', who published his *Hydriotaphia* in 1658. It dealt with the discovery of forty or fifty urns containing burnt bones in a field at Old Walsingham, Norfolk. Incidentally the author observed[12]: 'som Brittish Coynes of gold have been dispersedly found; And no small number of silver peeces near *Norwich*; with a rude head upon the obverse, and an ill formed horse on the reverse, with Inscriptions *Ic. Duro. T.* whether implying *Iceni, Durotriges, Tascia,* or *Trinobantes,* we leave to higher conjecture'. On which Sir John Evans, our main authority, remarks:[13] 'Browne's account of the silver coins probably struck by the Iceni...is both interesting and correct'. To be sure, Sir Thomas was not impeccable. He took those urns to be Roman. We know now that they were Saxon. But

[12] Ed. Sir J. Evans p. 25.   [13] *Ib.* p. xix.

stimulus of nascent Science—to realise that they lived in a very interesting world and that life, even local life, had a long history behind it. The Age of Antiquaries had arrived.

Their forerunner was Sir Thomas Browne, 'Doctour of Physick', who published his *Hydriotaphia* in 1658. It dealt with the discovery of forty or fifty urns containing burnt bones in a field at Old Walsingham, Norfolk. Incidentally the author observed[12]: 'som Brittish Coynes of gold have been dispersedly found; And no small number of silver peeces near *Norwich*; with a rude head upon the obverse, and an ill formed horse on the reverse, with Inscriptions *Ic. Duro. T.* whether implying *Iceni, Durotriges, Tascia,* or *Trinobantes*, we leave to higher conjecture'. On which Sir John Evans, our main authority, remarks:[13] 'Browne's account of the silver coins probably struck by the Iceni. . . is both interesting and correct'. To be sure, Sir Thomas was not impeccable. He took those urns to be Roman. We know now that they were Saxon. But

[12] Ed. Sir J. Evans p. 25. [13] *Ib.* p. xix.

who cares? We could forgive him anything in sheer gratitude for his quaint Latinisms and his rhetorical conceits. Just hear him speak:[14]

Now since these dead bones have already outlasted the living ones of *Methuselah*, and in a yard under ground, and thin walls of clay, out-worn all the strong and spacious buildings above it; and quietly rested under the drums and tramplings of three conquests; what Prince can promise such diuturnity unto his Reliques.... Time which antiquates Antiquities, and hath an art to make dust of all things, hath yet spared these *minor* Monuments. In vain we hope to be known by open and visible conservatories, when to be unknown was the means of their continuation and obscurity their protection.

Nine years later Sir Thomas returned to the topic and wrote a treatise on some urns—Roman urns this time—found near Brampton in Norfolk. The circumstances of the find are recorded with all the exactitude that a modern archaeologist would demand, though the illustration savours of a bygone day.

[14] *Op. cit.* p. 71.

Our Cambridge Antiquaries could not hope to rival Sir Thomas Browne's pomp of language, but they were at least capable of doing useful spade-work. County-histories, town-histories, cathedral-histories were very much in vogue, and both here and at Oxford an enormous amount of honest antiquarian research was carried out. Not all of it saw the light of day.[15] Thomas Baker, Fellow of St John's, at his death in 1740 left manuscript materials for a history of the University amounting to forty-two folio volumes: most of them are still unpublished. William Cole, of Clare and King's, in 1782 bequeathed an even bigger collection to the British Museum—a hundred folios on Cambridgeshire and the adjoining counties. The Antiquaries have been in turn abused and derided; but they did know how to work!

I must content myself with a single typical name. William Stukeley of Corpus was, like Sir Thomas Browne, *in primis* a medical

[15] H. G. Aldis in *The Cambridge History of English Literature* Cambridge 1912 ix. 354.

student. And he took his studies seriously. He matriculated in 1704, and—says he—[16]

I turned my mind particularly to the study of Physick, & in order thereto began to make a diligent & near inquisition into Anatomy & Botany, in consort with Hobart, a senior Lad of our College.... With him I went frequently a simpling, & began to steal dogs & dissect them & all sorts of animals that came in our way.... We had an old Cat in the house, which had been a great Favorite of my Fathers & the whole Familys, & by my Mothers leave I rid her of the infirmitys of age, & made a handsom sceleton of her bones....

Chemistry too claimed his attention, for he continues:[17]

This winter 1705 I went again to Chymical Lectures with Seignor Vigani at his Laboratory in Queen's College.... At this time my Tutor gave me a Room in the College to dissect in, & practise Chymical Experiments, which had a very strange appearance with my Furniture in it, the wall was generally hung round with Guts, stomachs, blad-

[16] W. Stukeley *Family Memoirs* (The Surtees Soc. i) 1882 p. 21.
[17] *Ib.* p. 33.

ders, preparations of parts & drawings. I had sand furnaces, Calots, Glasses & all sorts of Chymical Implements.... Here I & my Associats often dind upon the same table as our dogs lay upon. I often prepared the pulvis fulminans & sometime surprizd the whole College with a sudden explosion. I cur'd a lad once of an ague with it by a fright.

I get the impression that young Stukeley was a thorough scientist. But all the while there was within him an intense hankering for Classical Archaeology. He says:[18]

I learnt French about this Time...& designed to learn Italian for I had thoughts of travelling, especially to Rome which place I have ever had the most earnest desire of seeing, thinking there is all that can possibly satisfy the most curious Enquirer. That City, which has been the Residence of the Greatest Genius's that ever lived, firing my ambition to breath in Italian Air, & could only tempt me to undergoe the fatigues & dangers of foreign Expeditions where I might behold the Pantheon, the Pillars, the Obelisks, the Gates, the Amphitheaters, & all that Art has to boast of Great & Venerable. But my hopes were frustrate,

[18] *Op. cit.* p. 25.

& Imagination alone & Prints must supply the want of Real inspection; & had I gone 'tis not unlikely their Painting, Statuary, Music, their sober way of living, would have suited so well to my tast & constitution that I should have been content to pass my Life there. However, in some measure to allay my thirst at leisure hours, I drew out a whole paper book of the Antient & Modern Structures there, which I have still by me.

That is a pathetic page, written *ripae ulterioris amore*. But if Stukeley had to forego Italy, he could and did console himself with England. The habits of keen observation, fostered in the class-rooms of Cambridge, were turned to good account, when in after years he devoted himself to the investigation of his own country's past. Season after season he rode out with his friend Roger Gale, partly to search for antiquities, partly to stave off the gout.[19] In 1724 he published his *Itinerarium Curiosum*, which contains an account of these trapesings—Richborough, Dover, Bath, Dorchester, Old Sarum, and the rest. In 1725 he traversed the

[19] *Op. cit.* p. 51 f.

whole length of Hadrian's Wall and described it in detail.[20] He had an eye too for humbler monuments. He insisted that the turf-cut mazes of the country-side were well worthy of attention.[21] And, within two months of its discovery, he drew the Royston Cave—'Lady Roisia's Oratory' he called it—and made an accurate transcript of its remarkable carvings.[22] In 1740 came his most famous book *Stonehenge a Temple restor'd to the British Druids*, and three years later *Abury a Temple of the British Druids*. Stukeley (it must be admitted) had Druids on the brain. At Grantham he transformed his orchard into a sylvan copy of Stonehenge, retaining for its centre an old apple-tree overgrown with mistletoe.[23] Oddly enough, posterity has reverted to the idea that a Stonehenge presupposes a Woodhenge. Mr Newall, the latest writer on the subject, makes it probable that at the close of the Neolithic Age balks of timber stood in the 'Aubrey

[20] *Op. cit.* p. 52.   [21] Stukeley *Itin. Cur.* p. 91 ff.
[22] Stukeley *Palæographia Britannica* London 1743 No. 1, 1746 No. 2.
[23] Stukeley *Family Memoirs* p. 208 f.

holes'.[24] Sir Arthur Evans long since suggested that the original centre of Stonehenge was a sacred tree.[25] Mr Windle defined it as 'a sacred oak-tree'.[26] And now Mr Kendrick of the British Museum reaches the conclusion that Stonehenge, a circle dating from the Early Bronze Age, was during the La Tene period reconstructed and used as a druidic temple.[27] Be that as it may, Stukeley deserves all credit for his minutely accurate record of existing *data*. Even his grotesque-looking ground-plan of the giant rings at Avebury[28] has been verified by more recent measurements. At most we can object that head and tail were an absurd addition, due to his mistaken belief in *dracontia* or serpent-fanes. The fact is, Stukeley, like many a modern scholar, was scrupulous in his collection of evidence, but rash in his inter-

[24] R. S. Newall 'Stonehenge' in *Antiquity* 1929 iii. 75 ff.

[25] A. Evans 'Stonehenge' in *The Archaeological Review* 1889 ii. 327 ff.

[26] B. C. A. Windle *Remains of the Prehistoric Age in England* London 1904 p. 184.

[27] T. D. Kendrick *The Druids* London 1927 pp. 155 f., 209 f.

[28] R. Hippisley Cox *Where Green Roads meet* Swindon 1929 p. 24.

pretation of it. And on occasion his imaginings led him into error. A notorious case is his invention of the empress ORIVNA—a mere misreading of the word FORTVNA on a coin of Carausius.[29] On the other hand, Stukeley was sometimes right and his detractors wrong. Thomas Hearne in one of his letters says:[30]

This Dr S. is a mighty conceited man....He pretended to have discovered a Roman Amphitheatre at Silchester, a draught of the walls thereof he shewed me. This is again fancy. I have been at Silchester, there is nothing like it.

Mr Collingwood in his recent Handbook of *Roman Britain* enumerates its extant amphitheatres, and Silchester heads the list.[31]

But, right or wrong, Stukeley was a great character. Some months ago at David's bookstall on the market-place I picked up a small vellum-bound book in Stukeley's handwriting. It is entitled *Cambridg Ely Cotenham Diary*

[29] Stukeley *Palæographia Britannica* London 1747 No. 3 vignette on title-page.
[30] Stukeley *Family Memoirs* p. 170.
[31] R. G. Collingwood *The Archaeology of Roman Britain* London 1930 p. 106.

1736. A few pages are taken up with purely personal items:

> Murray pmisd me fome ro. coyns
> D: Harwood likew. & a ring & intagl.
> bargained wth Mr Lant to cut my
> hair 6 times in a year from
> 13. Mar. 1727–8 for 6^s pr ann...
> lent Mr Wyng S^r Is. Newtons
> Chronology 2. Oct. 1730.

Another page recalls his quaint orchard at Grantham. The whimsical Arthur-Rackham willow goes some way towards explaining the freakish head and tail of the Avebury serpent. And the lower entry, inverted, shows that the doctor kept up his undergraduate interests. It reads:

A dog lost much of his mettle and fierceness after spleen cut out.

Yet another page gives his sketch of a gem found in Anglesea. He calls it—of course—a Druid's head! But the most interesting portion of the little volume is concerned with the antiquities of Cambridge and its neighbourhood. Here is a sample. He had ridden out with

Roger Gale to visit Haddenham Church and St Audrey's Well:

a remarkable accident happend just before we were at Audrey. a traveller coming thither was taken ill of the small pox & dyd. when he was buryd, the country folks drove a flock of sheep quite thro' the house, with a notion that it would take the infection away. within 2 days after 9 familys in the town were siezd with the small pox, the sheep having carried it away with them.

You appreciate the combined interest (not to say humour) of the medical man and the antiquary. Both are often concerned in local folklore.

The age of Antiquaries was followed by the age of Travellers. Throughout the latter part of the eighteenth century and the early decades of the nineteenth it was becoming more and more the fashion to make the Grand Tour. This, no doubt, involved expense, fatigue, and a *modicum* of danger. But the game was worth the candle, and it was played with gusto. Among the risks to be run were brigandage by land and piracy by sea. We have to remember that throughout the whole of the seventeenth century Barbary pirates were a real menace to Mediterranean shipping, that in the course of the eighteenth they gradually declined, and that they were not finally put down till the French conquest of Algiers in 1830.[32] Small wonder, then, that in 1649 when Baron Craven by will founded the Craven Scholarships, he directed that the residue of his estate be devoted to the redemption of English captives at Algiers or any other place under the dominion of the Turk.[33] Cambridge scholars mostly succeeded in slipping through the fingers of the corsairs. But a sad tale is told of the French numismatist Vaillant, who himself gave the details to Spon the associate of George Wheler. Vaillant had been commissioned by Louis XIV to visit the Levant in search of coins for the royal cabinet. He travelled through Italy, Sicily, and Greece. But when, in 1674, he left Leghorn for Rome, he was captured by pirates and kept a prisoner at Algiers for

[32] *Enc. Brit.*[14] *s.v.* 'Barbary Pirates'.
[33] *University of Cambridge Historical Register* p. 259.

four months and a half. At last he was set at liberty, and even allowed to retain a score of gold coins and some 200 silver pieces found in his chest. But two days out from Algiers his ship was again chased by pirates. Vaillant in desperation left the silver coins to their fate and, piece by piece, swallowed the gold! At this point I abbreviate the narrative. The skill of two French surgeons sufficed for the recovery both of the gold and of its owner.[34]

Many marbles in our public and private collections doubtless came to this country as souvenirs of Italy and Greece. A fine head of Apollo was found at Ventnor in a cottage known to have been built by the Levantine traveller, Sir Richard Worsley. Five Greek tombstones, perhaps from Smyrna, were stacked in a store at Portsmouth. Another, seen at Athens in 1720, was unearthed below a house in New Bond Street.[35] A fragment of the

[34] E. Babelon *Traité de monnaies grecques et romaines* Paris 1901 i. 1. 138 n. 1 citing Spon *Voyage d'Italie* i. 9 f.
[35] *Brit. Mus. Cat. Sculpture* i nos. 211; 643, 652, 679, 726, 736; 667.

Parthenon frieze turned up in 1902 on a rockery at Colne Park, Essex.[36] And—I must add—twenty years ago Farmer Bull of Cottenham walked into our Museum and presented me with this beautiful relief of a young Greek leading his horse. The work, as I have argued elsewhere,[37] may be dated about 485 B.C. and, if so, is our best sculptured memorial of the men who fought at Marathon. But how came it to be found eighteen inches under the surface of a field at Cottenham? Presumably it was an isolated relic thrown out from a house long since demolished. Now Roger Gale (whose portrait by Lely hangs on the staircase of our University Library) is known to have had a manor-house at Cottenham in 1728, and his enthusiasm for 'Greek and Roman bustoes' is on record. Was this one of his treasures, dropped in the dust-bin as a broken bit of marble by some later Philistine?

Among the scholar-travellers of this University were Dodwell of Trinity, who published

[36] *Guide to the Sculptures of the Parthenon* p. 98.
[37] *Journ. Hell. Stud.* 1917 xxxvii. 116ff. pl. 1.

his *Tour through Greece* in 1819 and his *Views in Greece* with exquisite colour-plates in 1821; Morritt of St John's, who surveyed the Troad and stoutly defended the historicity of Homer; and Sir William Gell of Emmanuel, who popularised Pompeii and did so much to earn Byron's epithet 'rapid Gell'—had he not polished off his *Topography of Troy* in just three days and gone on to sketch 'one hundred routes' in Greece?

But our best known traveller was Dr E. D. Clarke of Jesus, who filled eleven volumes with his peregrinations from Egypt to Scandinavia. Having exhausted the surface of the ground, he devoted his attention to its constituents and became Professor of Mineralogy, in which capacity he invented (or helped to invent) the oxy-hydrogen blowpipe. He presented to the University the numerous sculptures that he had brought back from Greece, and these are now to be seen in the basement of the Fitzwilliam Museum. Conspicuous among them is the great marble *Kistophóros* from Eleusis.[38] Clarke

[38] *Zeus* i. 173 n. 1.

found it there in 1801, buried up to its neck in a dung-hill, not by way of contumely, but because the villagers regarded it with the utmost veneration. They believed that the fertility of their land depended on this sacred figure, and argued that manure meant for the fields must first be brought into contact with it. Clarke, having bribed the waiwode of Athens, purchased the statue and obtained a firman for its removal. But portents occurred. The very evening before it went, an ox butted into it and ran off bellowing into the plain of Eleusis. The peasants were aghast, and Clarke had to call in the local priest in full canonicals to deal the first blow with a pickaxe. Even then the people declared that no ship with their statue on board would ever get safe to port. And they were right. The *Princessa,* a merchantman bringing it home from Smyrna, was wrecked near Beachy Head. However, the statue was salved and in due course reached Cambridge. Its arrival was hailed as something of a triumph. But the whole business strikes me as frankly immoral. To rob the harmless villagers of their

fetish! I for one would have left it in its here-
ditary dunghill. Perhaps the best thing to be
said of Clarke is to recall his protest against
the restorer's art. He writes (and the date is
1809):[39]

No attempt has been made towards the restoration of any of the Marbles.... They have
been deposited in the Vestibule exactly as they
were found. In this respect we have not imitated
the example of the French: and it is believed, the
Public will not dispute the good taste of the
University, preferring a mutilated fragment of
Grecian sculpture, to any modern reparation. Had
Ceres gone to Paris, she would soon have issued
from a French toilet, not only with a new face,
but with all her appropriate insignia, her car,
dragons, and decorations, until scarce any of the
original Marble remained visible.

So Clarke very wisely contented himself with
a restoration of the face on paper by Flaxman.
   The most important outcome of classical
travel was, however, the foundation of the

   39 E. D. Clarke *Greek Marbles*...Cambridge 1809 p. ii f.
with Frontispiece.

Dilettanti Society. The Preface to one of their stately volumes says:[40]

In the year 1724, some gentlemen who had travelled in Italy, desirous of encouraging, *at home*, a taste for those objects which had contributed so much to their entertainment *abroad*, formed themselves into a Society, under the name of the DILETTANTI.

The primary object was undoubtedly that of a dinner-club; but the diners were to be men of talent interested in the promotion of art. At an earlier date they would have been called *virtuosi*, at a later date *amateurs*.[41] A painting by Sir Joshua Reynolds sufficiently indicates the twofold character of the Society, at once grave and gay. Sir William Hamilton is seated at a table, discussing the style of an ancient Greek wine-jug; six of his friends are grouped around, discussing the contents of its modern quivalent. Convivial or not, the Dilettanti had a splendid record. It is true that, under the bale-

[40] *Antiquities of Ionia* London 1821 i p. i.
[41] (Sir) Lionel Cust *History of the Society of Dilettanti* ed. Sir Sidney Colvin London 1914 p. 6f.

ful influence of Payne Knight and backed up by the indignation of Byron, they did their wickedest to discredit the Elgin marbles—their attack being eventually foiled by West and Fuseli and above all by that magnificent fighter Benjamin Robert Haydon. But it is also true that the Society produced a long series of monumental works, great slabs of books on which is built our knowledge of Greek Architecture—five folios on the *Antiquities of Athens*,[42] four on the *Antiquities of Ionia*.[43] William Wilkins of Caius, architect of Downing and translator of Vitruvius, was at work on yet another volume when he died in 1839. It says much for the value of the series that as late as 1915, in the mid stress of the War, Macmillan thought it worth while to publish the plates prepared by Wilkins more than 75 years before. Nor were these the only achievements of the Dilettanti. Chandler, and Penrose, and Cockerell are great names in Classical Archaeology. Their works were ren-

[42] *Antiquities of Athens* i–iv 1762–1816, v 1830.
[43] *Antiquities of Ionia* i–iii 1769–1840, iv 1881, v 1915.

dered possible by the support of the same powerful and generous Society.[44]

Meantime travel for serious, scientific purposes tended to develop into topography. The first sixty years of the nineteenth century might be called the Age of Topographers. First and foremost of them was Martin Leake, Lieutenant-Colonel in the Royal Artillery, who from 1800 to 1810 was constantly occupied in a survey of Asia Minor, Syria, Egypt, European Turkey, and Greece. The result was a sequence of scholarly books—*Researches in Greece*,[45] *The Topography of Athens*,[46] *Journal of a Tour in Asia Minor*,[47] *Travels in the Morea*,[48] *Travels in Northern Greece*,[49] *Peloponnesiaca*.[50] Sir William Ramsay speaks of 'his wonderful topographical eye and instinct',[51] nor is there much exaggeration in the epitaph at Kensal Green which calls him 'an unwearied searcher after

[44] A. Michaelis *Ancient Marbles in Great Britain* Cambridge 1882 p. 63 n. 160.
[45] 1814.   [46] 1821.   [47] 1824.
[48] 1830.   [49] 1835.   [50] 1846.
[51] W. M. Ramsay *Historical Geography of Asia Minor* London 1890 p. 97 f.

truth'.[52] Others who did good service along the same lines were Pashley of Trinity[53] and Vice-Admiral Spratt[54]—the latter in Lycia, and both of them in Crete.

Travellers and topographers were often collectors too. Leake presented his marbles to the British Museum; but his bronzes, vases, gems, and coins were purchased by Cambridge for £5000.[55] The bronzes include one or two specimens of importance; the vases, five artists' signatures; the gems, one masterpiece by Dexamenos. But the coins are of the greatest value, for Leake did not disdain mere coppers. He got them by the dozen; indeed, he found that in Thessaly and Macedonia such pieces regularly went into the melting-pot and were converted by the local copper-smith into kettles and caldrons![56]

[52] J. H. Marsden *A brief Memoir of...W. M. Leake* London 1864 p. 43.

[53] R. Pashley *Travels in Crete* 1837.

[54] T. A. B. Spratt *Travels in Lycia* 1847, *Travels and Researches in Crete* 1865.

[55] A. Michaelis *op. cit.* p. 267.

[56] J. H. Marsden *op. cit.* p. 23.

John Disney, founder of the Disney Professorship, bequeathed to Cambridge a large collection of sculpture. Thomas Worsley, Master of Downing, did the same on a smaller scale. Other notable collections were the engraved gems of C. W. King, dispersed by sale, and the vases, gems, and coins of Samuel Savage Lewis, bequeathed to Corpus, where they are now so worthily installed and tended.

But I have reached living memory and can afford to shorten my story. By the middle of the century *Antiquaries, Travellers, Topographers, Collectors* had all contributed their quota and largely done their work. It was time for some fresh stimulus to make itself felt. And the fresh stimulus came, as it always has come, from renewed contact with Mother Earth. The thirty years between 1850 and 1880 fairly inaugurated the Age of *Excavators*, which has lasted on to our own day. Ludolf Stephani opened up tumulus after tumulus in the Crimea and recovered a brilliant and barely suspected chapter in the border-history of Greeks and

Scythians. Mariette cleared the Serapeum at Memphis from its thick stratum of sand and excavated a whole series of temples at Edfu, Dendera, Karnak, Deir-el-Bahari. Smith and Porcher explored the district of Cyrene. Sir Charles Newton at Halikarnassos, at Knidos, at Branchidai unearthed and carried off an amazing wealth of Greek sculpture, and posed problems in Greek architecture that still await their final solution. Others were equally active in Asia Minor and the Archipelago—Humann in Samos and at Pergamon, Pullan at Teos and Priene, Salzmann and Biliotti in Rhodes, Lebègue in Delos. In Italy Fiorelli was digging at Pompeii, Pietro Rosa on the Palatine. And almost simultaneously the pile-dwellings of Switzerland and the rock-shelters of southern France began to reveal their secrets. In fact, N. S. E. and W., furrows for a fresh harvest were being busily ploughed.[57]

But the excavator's art is not learnt in a day, and many of these enterprises were unmetho-

[57] A. Michaelis *A Century of Archaeological Discoveries* London 1908, p. 344 ff. and Index.

dical and superficial. General Cesnola, as American Consul in Cyprus, rifled hundreds (not to say thousands) of tombs, but dispensed with personal supervision and seldom made notes on the spot. Dodging the Turkish officials, he left the island with some 35,000 exhibits, most of which were bought by the Metropolitan Museum of New York: they had to wait forty years before they were properly classified and published.[58] J. T. Wood was sent out by the British Museum and the Dilettanti to locate the Artemision at Ephesos, which had vanished in the marshy ground. After six years' search he did find it, exactly where Kiepert thirty years earlier had predicted that it would be found. Wood's excavation was protracted and badly mismanaged. His handsome quarto does not even give us a reliable ground-plan, though it runs to colour-plates of a Roman mosaic and a Turkish brigand! The thing was a scandal. Indeed, Middleton told me that once, when he had

[58] J. L. Myres *Handbook of the Cesnola Collection* New York 1914 p. xiv ff.

been fulminating about it, his dragoman came to him privately and said: 'Shall I shoot him for you, sir?' Worse still was the work of the Epirote banker Karapanos, who claimed to have discovered Dodona—though it had long since been identified by the architect Donaldson. After five months' unsuccessful digging, done by somebody else, Karapanos purchased miscellaneous antiques at *Yanina* and proceeded to publish *Dodone et ses ruines* with 63 choice plates.[59] Of course, to seek is not always to find. Better men than Karapanos were not wholly successful. Schliemann believed that his life's dream had come true, when at long last he reached *Hissarlik*. But, though he actually dug into that wonderful hill, he failed to find the stratum that alone corresponds with Homer's Troy. Even the Germans at Olympia, whose great work still ranks as the ideal publication of a classical site, missed the earliest settlement and left much for Dörpfeld to glean in the very heart of the Altis.

The cure for all these ills was in sight when

[59] Michaelis *op. cit.* p. 134.

Archaeology began to be scientific. Round about the year 1880 classical students, largely under the pressure of contemporary Science, awoke to the fact that real progress demanded stricter methods, more exact observation, better-kept records, more active coöperation, more enlightened criticism, more definite and systematic training. Archaeology must be organised. And organised it was—not on any comprehensive plan imposed by Government, but (as suits our national mood) by collective and individual effort of a more sporadic kind.

In 1879 the Society for the promotion of Hellenic Studies was founded. Its originator was Dr George Macmillan. In company with Prof. Sayce he drew up a list of 120 persons, who had actually visited Greece, and invited them to join the proposed Society. When, two years ago, that Society celebrated its jubilee, it could boast nearly 1400 members and 150 student-associates. Moreover, Dr Macmillan, with fifty years' service to his credit, was still acting as its Honorary Secretary. It is hard to overestimate the debt that we owe to him.

One of the earliest tasks undertaken by the Society was to issue the now famous *Journal of Hellenic Studies,* which has appeared with unbroken regularity ever since the year 1880. The Society has also published Supplementary Papers and facsimiles of important Manuscripts. Its rooms in London, within easy reach of the British Museum, form a convenient *focus* for workers, who there have access to a large and admirably-catalogued collection of books, and photographs, and slides.

If it was an Oxford man who founded the Hellenic Society, it was a Cambridge man who fathered the British School at Athens. In 1878 Prof. Jebb wrote an article for the *Contemporary Review* propounding a scheme for the establishment of such a School. In 1882 he submitted his scheme to the Council of the Hellenic Society, which however was not then willing to take action. But Jebb was not to be put off. Returning to the charge in 1883, he sent to the *Fortnightly Review* 'A Plea for a British Institute at Athens'. A big meeting was held at Marlborough House, attended by

Mr Gladstone, Lord Salisbury, and grandees galore. They resolved to start the School, and it was formally opened in October 1886.

It should be added that relations between the British School at Athens and the Hellenic Society in England have, from the first, been most cordial. After all, they are not so much rival companies as a field-force abroad and its base at home. Even the publication of a School *Annual* from 1895 onwards has in practice proved more of a help than a hindrance to the sale of the Society's *Journal*.[60]

After Greece, Italy. The British School at Rome, projected in 1899, was opened in the spring of 1901, got to work at once, and issued the first of its *Papers* in 1902. Seven years later its Committee, having talked things over with representatives of the Classical Association and with the Council of the Hellenic Society, recommended that a new Society be established for the promotion of Roman Studies. It held its first meeting in June 1910 and published its

[60] G. A. Macmillan in the *Journ. Hell. Soc.* 1929 xlix 'An Outline of the History of the Hellenic Society' p. ii ff.

first *Journal* in 1911. That year the Romans became tenants of the Hellenes; and, ever since, the two Societies have lived and laboured amicably under the same roof.[61]

The new ferment of Classical Archaeology early began to leaven the old Universities. The Fitzwilliam Museum Syndicate, with the sanction of the Senate, contributed no less than £7500 for building galleries of Greek sculpture. The University added another £2000 for adjoining galleries to house its antiquarian and ethnological collections. A site was secured on a 99-years lease from Peterhouse. This involved the demolition of an old malting-house and the reconstruction of a big warehouse. And so the Museum, in which we are met today, came to be. At the inaugural proceedings on May 6, 1884 Prof. Colvin, speaking in this room, said:

It would be affectation in me not to acknowledge that the scheme has been in great part mine, and that for the merits or demerits of its execution I am personally to a large extent responsible. Ever since I came back to live and work here it has

[61] Statement prefixed to the *Journ. Rom. Stud.* 1911 i.

been the one thing I cared most to see done: and now, well or ill, it is done.[62]

Sir Sidney Colvin might indeed look back with pride on the accomplishment of his project. As Slade Professor he had been virtually the first to attempt any systematic teaching of Classical Archaeology. And he had been hopelessly hampered by sheer lack of apparatus. A few casts in the Fitzwilliam basement were available to illustrate special lectures. But they were quite insufficient even for that limited purpose. And now, thanks to his personal exertions and those of Mr J. W. Clark (then President of the Antiquarian Society), he found himself equipped with 633 Casts[63] and a Library of Archaeological books that in this country at least had no equal.

At the same time it must be confessed that the new venture started under two disabilities. It was, in a sense, both burdened and itself a burden. It was burdened by being somewhat unequally yoked with the Museum of General

[62] *Cambridge University Reporter* 1883–1884 p. 966.
[63] *Ib.* 1884–1885 p. 891.

Archaeology. And it was itself a burden to the Fitzwilliam fund, which not only was depleted to build this Museum, but had for many years to contribute the annual sum of £500 towards its upkeep. These anomalies (to use no harsher term) were rectified in due course. In 1912 the Galleries occupied by General Archaeology were left vacant, their contents having been removed to the new Museum of Archaeology and Ethnology.[64] The Buildings Syndicate then took in hand the needed structural alteration and redecoration of the whole Museum.[65] The Cast Collection, by that time suffering badly from congestion, obtained more breathing-space, and the Old Library was supplemented by a larger and much more convenient room. Simultaneously a new scheme of management, involving the separate administration of the Fitzwilliam Museum and the Museum of Classical Archaeology, had come into force and was working well—though the drain upon

[64] *Cambridge University Reporter* 1912–1913 : Report of Committee 5 Dec. 1912.
[65] *Ib.* 1912–1913 p. 1156.

the Fitzwilliam fund continued for another ten years. [66]

A word must here be said in grateful memory of Sir John Sandys, who from 1911 to 1921, the critical period of transition, presided over the Museum Committee with judgment, energy, and tact. During his life-time he made repeated gifts to the Library, and after his death these benefactions were continued on a generous scale by Lady Sandys. The number of books in the Museum was thus brought up to a total of nearly 9000, necessitating the formation of a new Card Catalogue.

One other change recommended by the Buildings Syndicate of 1912 is still in abeyance. They proposed to demolish the small tenements built into the Museum and to extend the north Gallery in their place. That, mark you, is a course to which the University is definitely committed by the terms of its lease with Peterhouse. The extension, repeatedly advocated by the Museum Committee, becomes

[66] *Cambridge University Reporter* 1922–1923 p. 288, 1923–1924 p. 566.

year by year more urgently needful. The number of Casts to be accommodated has risen from 633 to 825, and the end is not yet. Ultimately, when the lease falls in, it may be found necessary to migrate and go further afield. For no limits can, or should, be set to the normal process of growth.

But it takes more than bricks and mortar to build up a School like ours. Equipment, of course, means something. The human element means more. I shall spend my remaining minutes best, if I remind you of certain outstanding personalities who for long years bore the burden of teaching and the heat of controversy on our behalf. It is to them that we are mainly indebted for the record of this School—successful doings on a dozen different sites in Greece and Italy; and those who know Cambridge will realise how much of their generous labours went without recognition or reward.

When I entered this place as a student, over forty years ago, the teaching was carried on by the Reader Charles Waldstein (later Sir

Charles Walston) and the Slade Professor John Henry Middleton.

Waldstein was of Austrian descent, but born in New York and educated in Heidelberg, where he took his degree in philosophy, classical archaeology, and international law.[67] The result was a man of broadly cosmopolitan views with a special bent for philosophy. It was in fact as an ethical teacher that he first came here at the invitation of Henry Sidgwick. I once heard him join issue with Lord Balfour on a point of ethics. After the War he roughed out a 'Philosophy of Harmonism'[68] (though nobody showed much inclination to live by it), and he embodied his ideas on politics in a book called *Aristodemocracy*.[69] Later he lectured on eugenics, civics, and ethics to a Cambridge congress.[70] This strain of abstract thinking runs

[67] Sir C. Walston *Alcamenes* Cambridge 1926 p. vii.

[68] *Cambridge University Reporter* 1920–1921 pp. 212, 296, 554, 894. Cp. Sir C. Walston *Harmonism and conscious Evolution* London 1922.

[69] Sir C. Walston *Aristodemocracy* London 1916.

[70] Sir C. Walston *Eugenics, Civics, and Ethics* Cambridge 1920.

through all his published work. In Archaeology it was at once his strength and his weakness. It enabled him to compare and contrast on the grand scale. But it made him impatient of detail and the verification of minor matters. Joined with his philosophical temperament was a sensitive appreciation of Art. His judgments were subjective, but commonly sound; for he had the seeing eye. Rhythm and symmetry and anything that spelt, or even misspelt, Hellenic perfection he loved. Rodin, I think, he excused.[71] He would have hated Epstein. It was not the *Genesis* but the *Revelation* of beauty that he worshipped, and stamped in gold on the cover of his latest volume was the exquisite head from Bologna. I remember him best as a lecturer on Sculpture—prolix, polysyllabic, on occasion plethoric, but always persuasive and not seldom convincing. One point he rightly stressed, the need to see things in the round, not only on the flat. Hence he made great play with the plaster Casts—a habit that the friendly

[71] Sir C. Walston *Greek Sculpture and Modern Art* Cambridge 1914 *passim*.

caricaturist was not slow to satirise.[72] Yet caricature, after all, is a species of compliment. And Sir Charles Walston was undeniably a help to his generation.

His colleague was a man of widely different type. If Walston was an idealist with a gift for fancies, Middleton was a realist with a grasp of facts. As an architect and the son of an architect he loved definite lines and exact numbers, though he allowed himself a certain latitude in his treatment of non-essentials. Above all he keenly relished technical processes, and he made us relish them too. The curvature of a stylobate, the setting out of an Ionic volute, the use of *Pozzolana* in hydraulic cement, the *cire perdue* method of bronze-casting—these things appealed to the craftsman in his veins. Even greater was his interest in any material problem: How came Eupalinos to start his tunnel in Samos from opposite sides of the mountain and to meet so nearly in the middle? How did the old gem-engravers manage without a lens, or had they after all a

72 H. G. J[ones] *Friends in Pencil* Cambridge 1893 p. 9.

drop of water in a wire loop? And what about those minute Egyptian mosaics? Were they really made of glass rods arranged in a pattern, fused, drawn out, and cut in slices, like a modern sugar-stick? Or ancient bowls of *mille-fiore* glass—were they identical with our own gewgaws? I recall the joy with which he dwelt on early Etruscan granulated gold. Castellani[73] had found a man still making it in a remote village of the Apennines, had carried him in triumph to Rome, and (added Middleton *more suo*) killed him with hotel dinners. But Castellani had learnt his secret, and himself produced fair imitations of it. And then Castellani had died without divulging the method! Ready of the British Museum was labouring in vain to recapture the lost art. Middleton must have seen many things.[74] He had been in Iceland with William Morris. He had crossed the Rockies to Salt Lake City and stalked Digger Indians in California. He had visited Morocco

[73] M. A. Castellani *A Memoir on the Jewellery of the Ancients* p. 5 f.

[74] (Sir) Lionel Cust in the *Dictionary of National Biography* London 1901 Suppl. iii. 166 f.

and had penetrated the Great Mosque at Fez, disguised as a pilgrim. He had been imprisoned in Arabia, where he shared the cell of a cut-throat and fished for cheese and black-olives from the prison-window. If any man knew his Rome, it was Middleton. He knew it above ground, and he knew it below ground—he had ventured in a boat up the *Cloaca Maxima*, getting his direction (so he said) from the rumble of the traffic overhead. Even the Germans were glad to 'pirate' his Map of the *Forum*. He contributed no fewer than 82 articles to the *Encyclopaedia Britannica*⁹![75] One of these was expanded into a book on *Ancient Rome*[76] and finally issued in two volumes.[77] Middleton proposed to follow this up with a book on *Medieval Rome*; which remained un-written, for his thoughts were diverted to Athens and fresh labours intervened.[78] I am

[75] J. S. C[otton] in *The Academy* 20 June 1896 p. 514.

[76] J. H. Middleton *Ancient Rome in 1885* Edinburgh 1885, *id. Ancient Rome in 1888* Edinburgh 1888.

[77] J. H. Middleton *The Remains of Ancient Rome* London and Edinburgh 1892.

[78] J. T. M. in *The Athenæum* 20 June 1896 p. 817.

not likely to forget my first visit to Greece with Middleton for guide and for companions John Black, editor of the *Encyclopaedia,* and James Frazer, then at work on his *Pausanias.*

Middleton was a born teacher. But neither he nor Walston was a classical scholar. Sir William Ridgeway was. He had been Greek Professor at Cork, and to the end of his life he never ceased to maintain that Literature must come first. Hear how he puts it in his pamphlet on *The Relation of Archæology to Classical Studies.* He says:[79]

As it is the literature of Greece and Rome which is the eternal element, and as no study of classical archæology can have any real value unless it is based upon a sound knowledge of the literature and language, we may at once lay down that archæology in our educational system, both at school and in the university, must be regarded as ancillary to the study of the great writers of antiquity. Thus conceived and thus treated, archæology becomes an invaluable servant, for it enables us to grasp the meaning of the ancient writers, to

[79] W. Ridgeway *The Relation of Archæology to Classical Studies* p. 7 f.

comprehend allusions otherwise obscure, to en-
hance our enjoyment of the scenes which they de-
scribe, and to realise, in a way impossible for the
mere pedant, the conditions under which the
ancients lived and moved and had their being.

There speaks your genuine classic; and I, for
one, agree with every word. But how broad
must have been the sympathies and abilities of
the man if, feeling as he felt, he yet took his
doctorate in Science, not in Letters, on the
strength of his researches into *The Origin and
Influence of the thoroughbred Horse*.[80] Ridgeway
specialised in *Origins*. He wrote important
papers on the 'origin' of the 'Homeric Talent',[81]
'The Origin of the Stadion',[82] 'The Origin of
Jewellery',[83] 'The Origin of the Turkish Cres-
cent',[84] 'The Origin of the Indian Drama',[85]
and still more important books on *The Origin*

[80] Cambridge 1905.

[81] *Journ. Hell. Stud.* 1887 viii. 133 ff.

[82] *Ib.* 1887 ix. 18 ff.

[83] *Report of the British Association* 1903 London 1904
p. 815 f.

[84] *Journal of the Royal Anthropological Institute* 1908
xxxviii. 241 ff.

[85] *Journal of the Royal Asiatic Society* 1917.

of Metallic Currency and Weight Standards[86] and *The Origin of Tragedy*.[87] When the phrase palled, he varied it by a question and asked: 'What People produced the Objects called Mycenean?'[88]—'Why was the Horse driven before it was ridden?'[89]—'Who were the Dorians?'[90]—'Who were the Romans?'[91] Clearly his was the restless enquiring mind, not content to accept tradition, still less authority. Isolated and independent to a fault, he often ignored the work of foreign investigators. It might have been thought that this disdain of Teutonic *Litteratur*, for which he had little taste or talent, would have proved a fatal drawback to a scholar even of his calibre. In point of fact, it did not. Rather, it served to draw the fire of indignant critics, and Cambridge has more than once witnessed the heartening spectacle of Ridgeway *contra mundum*.

[86] Cambridge 1892.   [87] Cambridge 1910.
[88] *Journ. Hell. Stud.* 1896 xvi. 77 ff.
[89] *The Academy* 1891.
[90] *Anthropological Essays presented to E. B. Tylor* Oxford 1907 p. 295 ff.
[91] *Proceedings of the British Academy* London 1907 iii. 1 ff.

Provocative originality was one secret of his success as a teacher. But that was not all. A man may be original and provocative, or at least provoking, and yet the merest crank. Ridgeway's speculation was always sane, because based on a wide knowledge of human nature. His physical eyesight was dim, but his mind with compensatory clearness kept a broad and healthy outlook on the world at large. Hence his life-long devotion to the Study of Man and his fellow-feeling for its great exponents—Tylor, Robertson Smith, Frazer. Whether he lectured on Religion, or Coinage, or Gems, he did so always with reference to Greeks and Barbarians alike. Indeed, he frankly regarded Archaeology as a subsection of Anthropology.[92]

But I have said enough. Ridgeway was far too big a man to be packed into a penultimate paragraph. If any here had the misfortune not to know him, let them read the noble tribute paid to his memory by an old pupil, the present

[92] W. Ridgeway *The Relation of Archæology to Classical Studies* p. 1.

Regius Professor of Greek, and they will understand something of the impression that Ridgeway made upon us all:

In a Cambridge crowd (says Professor Robertson)[93] he looked like a stranger from some older and mightier race, one whose sword not ten men of modern breed could lift; and in the last year or two, when his health was visibly failing,...he moved through the streets like an old lion. But his high courage and fiery spirit were unquenchable, and rash disputants quickly learnt that ''tis better playing with a lion's whelp than with an old one dying'.

Walston, Middleton, Ridgeway—these were the men who in the main had the making of our School. And grave indeed is the responsibility of one who, without their powers, is attempting to carry on their work. Nevertheless, in the very diversity of their attainments I find some comfort. If past teachers have taught us anything, it is the manysidedness and complexity of the subject that we in our turn are professing to teach. Inevitably so. For Classical

[93] D. S. R[obertson] in *The Cambridge Review* 15 October 1926 p. 12.

Archaeology is nothing less than the attempt mentally to reconstruct, at least in its outward and material aspects, a whole bygone civilisation. Of course no one man is equal to the task. Such a pretension would recall the delegate from a Western University who, in the early days of the British Association, described himself as Professor of Science. No, the most we can hope to accomplish is to cultivate intensively some single patch, and to know our way about the remainder of the field well enough to appreciate our neighbour's crops. It is a case for conjoint effort and friendly collaboration. Pursuing it in this spirit, we shall find the subject growing and spreading under our hand. I anticipate that some day this University will feel bound to establish a Chair of Roman, as distinct from Greek, Archaeology, and Readerships in more than one outlying direction. Already there is much to be said for the creation of a Reader in Numismatics, and a no less urgent need for a Reader in British Archaeology.

Projects of this kind may, to some timorous

souls, especially in an hour of national stress, seem quite chimerical. But *are* they? We are here tonight to commemorate a great-hearted benefaction, inspired by sheer love of the Classics and marked by a wise recognition of their complexity. This signal encouragement, amid much talk of loss and limitation, comes to cheer us like a rainbow when storms are threatening. Let us accept the omen and push on with the work.

Printed in the United States
By Bookmasters